Why Now is the Right Time to Start a Business!
How to Beat the Odds and Be Successful!
Turn Your Dreams into Reality!

©2019 by Russell DeBord

All rights reserved.

Edition

Reproduction or translation of this product without the permission of the author is prohibited.

This publication is designed to provide accurate information and is based on the personal knowledge and experience of the author. It is to be understood that the information provided is not to be construed as legal or professional advice. You should seek the advice of a competent professional before moving forward on any personal endeavors.

Your Higher Desire, LLC

11040 E Quartet Ave. Mesa, Arizona 85212

YourHigherDesire.com

Today's world seems to move faster than ever. We don't have as much time to do the things we would like to do. There's not enough time in a day to accomplish what we set out to do in the morning.

Therefore, this book is purposefully written as a short book so that you can read it in one sitting, able to read in less than two hours for most readers. It is also written in simple, easy to follow terms so that it's easy to understand and more comprehensible. It's written to help you get motivated and to help overcome any fears you may have about starting a new business of your own. I only wish I had something like this short book available to me when I first contemplated starting a business. If so, I would have started my own business years sooner.

When you finish reading this book, I would appreciate it very much if would write a review for me. Reviews are the lifeblood of the writing industry, whether positive or negative. We authors learn what the readers think about our creations and hope to improve our works in the future. This is possible when we get feedback from you and you play a role in our next creation.

So please, feel free to leave a review! https://www.amazon.com/dp/B07RHVVLCX

Thank You!

P.S. Please visit my website for more!   www.yourhigherdesire.com

Table of Contents

Introduction

Stepping Out on Your Own

Financial Security

Sense of Purpose

Helping Others

Information at Your Fingertips

Let's Talk About Statistics

Owning a Home-Based Business

You Can Do It!

Using Your Talent

Let's Review What We've Been Talking About

What's next?

About the Author

Introduction

There is no better time to become self-reliant than right now. It used to be that a person could graduate from school and get a job and stay with that job for years and years and even until retirement. They could earn a nice pension from the company they worked for and live in retirement with enough income to live comfortably.

Those days are long gone. Nowadays you can earn a degree and be lucky to find a job as a gardener if you chose the wrong field of study. You could also have a student loan of thousands of dollars that needs to be paid off — not a very good way to start your life.

Even if you got a degree in a field that is in high demand, there is no guarantee that you would work for a company for more than a few years. If there's anything that we all know, it's that things change very rapidly in this world that we live in. What is in high demand now could change in an instant and the skills that you have now may be outdated in just a couple of years.

There is heavy competition for good jobs and skill levels are harder to keep current with the changing times. Younger people are coming out of the universities with new ideas, and it's more difficult to keep up.

That brings us back to what could be the best move for you to do - start a business of your own! Everybody has their own set of skills and talents. I would bet that you have the knowledge and experience that nobody else has. You have your own set of passions and desires. You have a way about you that nobody else does.

The trick is to develop an idea that exploits that talent and desire that only you have. And it really isn't even a trick. It's just expanding your horizons and letting the world know what it is that you can do and especially what you can do for them. You see, it's not even what you know that matters, it's putting what you know into action that will help them, your future customer.

That's the crazy thing; people don't really care about you or what you know; they just care about what they can get from you. In other words, what they are saying is "what's in it for me?" It's getting to be a really selfish world.

People are skeptical about anything and everything anymore and with good reason. A lot of people are deceptive and crooked. They steal and cheat. They pretend to be somebody they are not, gain your confidence and then steal your identity and rob you blind taking everything you have ever worked for including your retirement funds.

It's not very easy to build up a reputation for yourself or gain the confidence of another person. It takes work, and it takes time.

And yet the bottom line of your future customer is still "What's in it for me?" What can you do for me? What kind of service am I going to get? Can you really deliver? Are you going to do what you say you are going to do? Will that product really work? Is it worth it? How much will it cost me? Can I afford it? And most importantly, Can I trust you?

Answer these questions, and you are well on your way.

Getting back to our topic, why now is a good time to start a business. You can easily see that times have changed and that you can't rely on somebody else to achieve what you want out of life. You can't rely on working for a company as a means of security. Things change rapidly, and you could lose your job at any time for any reason.

You could be falsely accused of something and lose your job. You could say something that isn't politically correct and lose your job. You could look at somebody the wrong way and lose your job. It doesn't take much, and you'll be sent down the road.

And it may not even be your fault that you lose your job. Companies large and small seem to be downsizing all the time, and a lot of people lose their jobs. New technology comes along, and your job becomes obsolete, you're not needed anymore. Some companies make bad decisions and wind up in bankruptcy, and everybody loses their job. Or, the bosses daughter moves back home and winds up with your job. There are many ways that people lose their job, whether it's their own fault or because of reasons beyond their circumstances.

So what do you do? Too much reliance on somebody else could be detrimental to your livelihood. Although, working for somebody else is not totally bad either. You gain valuable knowledge of how the business system operates. If you pay attention to how the business you work for operates, you may notice a few ways on how that business can be more efficient. You may notice how they are not using their resources to capture a comparable market. You might know some other businesses that could use their service. Make a mental note of it.

You may see some missed opportunities that the business you are working for now is not taking advantage of. This is where a door opens, and there could be a good reason for you to start out on your own or maybe with a partner. It may be a great time for you to take these missed opportunities and create a business of your own.

Stepping Out on Your Own

You have learned the basics of your industry and may also have some advanced knowledge about the inside functionality of this business that nobody else has. That is how new opportunities are realized by many people that have started their own business, and they have become very successful. They not only become successful, but they also earn more money and live a life that has more personal security for them.

Most anybody can start a business of their own. It does take some discipline and drive and motivation to get started. But there are no limitations that can hold you back. You can be a man or a woman. You can be Black, White, Hispanic or any other nationality. You can be Christian, Jewish, Hindu, Buddist, Muslim or other any other faith. Many parents become business owners. I'm sure we've heard the expression of being a "work at home mom." It doesn't matter if you are gay, straight, or transgender. There are no restrictions on who can become the owner of a small business.

Those are some pretty good reasons to start your own business, but there's more to it than that. To become a good business, you need to fulfill the needs of others, whether it's fulfilling the needs of an individual or fulfilling the needs of another business. You can do it by providing a product or providing a service.

You can start a company that produces a product that can be sold to individuals or other businesses. Your product can be an improvement of a different product that is already on the market. A lot of businesses improve a product and sell it themselves. It is referred as "building a better mousetrap."

You could start a company that provides a service to individuals or other businesses. Sometimes this is referred to as B2C, business-to-customer or B2B, business-to-business.

Whether you start a business producing a product or providing a service is entirely up to you. They each have their advantages and disadvantages. To provide a product, you need to make sure that there is a demand for the product. You may already know that there is a demand because you can see the demand in your industry because you already have experience in that industry and if all you are doing is improving a particular product, then you can become very successful.

You will need to make a prototype of the product with specific directions on how it is produced. There are companies out there that can help you develop and test your prototype. For help, you can find developers at www.thomasnet.com. You need to make sure that there are no patents on it already and apply for your own patent to protect your interests. There are patent attorney's that you can hire to accomplish this. Go through these steps, and you are on your way to running your own business.

You can also go the route of providing a service to individuals or other businesses. There are many services needed by others whether it's as simple as providing a cleaning service, painting service, landscaping or bookkeeping or accounting services.

As you can see, there are many different fields in which a business can be created. Pick the one that appeals to you most and one in which you have talent. It's much easier to maintain a business if you have a passion for it too. You stay motivated and enthusiastic when you have a natural interest in the business you choose to start. It's also much easier to keep a business going if you have experience in it.

You don't want to start a business in which you have no experience or desire. What's the use in that? The learning curve would be tremendous, and if you have no desire, then it would be like going to prison each day. Neither one is practical or even feasible. So just because there is a lot of money in a particular field, it doesn't mean that you start a business in that area. That would be a big mistake. You would spend a lot of time and energy trying to learn something, and if you have no experience, then you would probably get wiped out by the competition.

It's best to go with something you know. It just makes sense.

With technology being the way that it is, everything is at your fingertips to help you with your endeavor. Most all the information you need is available at will. The computer can be your best friend when it comes to getting something, whether it's the latest statistics that you need to choose which direction you want to proceed in your business or getting products for your office. Or from getting receipt books or invoice forms to ordering a product from China. You can use technology to your advantage.

Financial Security

One of the most important reasons for starting your own business is to attain financial security. Businesses are in business to make money. If they don't make money, then they go out of business. Making money may not be the highest priority of a business. Providing a product or service is considered to be the highest priority. After all, that is how you earn money. Money is used as compensation for providing a product or service.

It's considered an exchange of one thing for another. We place value on our time and expense of providing a product. We place value on our time and experience when providing a service. A dollar value is put into place to determine what a fair trade would be. When both sides agree, then a transaction is made. In other words, that is how capitalism works. Capitalism may not be as bad as some people would have you believe.

Getting back to financial security, when you conduct business and have transactions you make money and if you are better at it than your competition, then you will attract more business and earn more money. The more you earn, the more you can invest and provide security for your future.

You can invest money back into your business. You can hire people to work for you. You can develop new products and create more business. You can expand into other locations or even franchise your business. There are many opportunities to grow and expand.

It all starts with investing in yourself. By putting time and effort into something that you enjoy, you can create your own opportunities. Be aware of your surroundings, and you may discover a way to capitalize on a situation that puts you in charge and on the way to financial freedom.

Sense of Purpose

As I mentioned earlier, we all have different experiences and different desires in life. We all have different passions, and we develop a particular knowledge about those passions. We acquire skills that become second nature to us. There are others that may become interested in the same things that we do. This is where a door can open that allows you to help the other person learn about your passion. You can teach them and earn money when you teach. This gives you income, and more importantly, you feel good about yourself because you are the one that helped this other person pursue a dream of theirs. This adds purpose to your life.

When you add purpose to your life, you live a fulfilling life. To help people is very rewarding. Your whole outlook on life becomes more positive. You smile more and live a happy life. When you are happy, people notice and they are more apt to be happy too. Sounds all soft and fuzzy, doesn't it?

Well, when you have a positive outlook on your life, and you help other people become successful in theirs, then yes your life becomes what some people might say - warm and fuzzy. When you enjoy helping others accomplish their dreams and get paid while doing it, you can't help but feel a sense of accomplishment. The people you help have nothing but praise for you.

Word gets out, and you become the go-to source on the subject. That is when even more doors open up for you to take advantage of. But you're not literally taking advantage of people; they are happy that you are there to help them. You are the one that helped them realize their dreams and are grateful you helped them achieve something that they had only dreamed about. You are the answer they had sought for perhaps years.

Sometimes, or more like most times, it's best to target people in the beginning stages of their quest. When people don't know anything or very little about something, and you have a lot of experience and knowledge about that topic, then there is an opportunity for you. You can become their source on how to help them achieve the skills that they need. They need to learn from somebody, so why not you? They will pay you for knowledge and skill. You can earn some extra money, or you can start a new career as a teacher, coach, consultant, or mentor.

For you, it can be easy money. It means you are trading your experience and talent to help somebody acquire the skills that you already possess. You can earn a nice income and perhaps financial security. You can find others that also want learn from you and multiply your income and security.

You can help people achieve their goals, dreams, and aspirations. When you are there for them, they are willing to pay handsomely for your efforts and advice. You can become their advisor. That could even lead to a recurring income which means you receive it week after week or month after month.

You may even start to have a following, and you'll be helping even more people achieve their dreams and goals. Your efforts can snowball to where you can have a team put together to help even more people. You can be proud of the way that you were able to help many people move forward with their own lives and that you were the spark to set forth a movement that makes this whole world better, one person at a time.

This can happen to you. If you pay attention to what is happening in your field of expertise and you see a demand or an interest develop, you can create a business around it. You can become the person that people will seek to learn more about what you already know. You can teach them and start a business around it.

Helping Others

A successful business is a business that helps others. That is what has become the most fruitful way for a business to succeed. When you give of yourself in a way that helps another person succeed, then you are successful yourself. You build up a good reputation for helping somebody in need.

Gone are the days when you could take short-cuts and get away with it. You may be able to get away with something for awhile but not for long. With the internet out there, word gets around really fast. If you try to cheat somebody, the word will get out fast, and you'll soon be out of business before it even gets off the ground.

The same goes if you try to charge too much for your service or product. It's so easy for people to shop around and find something for less money. It's easy for people to check you out before they even hire you. If you have a bad track record from bad reviews about you, you will quickly be passed by.

The only way to run a business is to be upfront and honest. When you are truthful and honest, you don't have to worry about what you may have done in the past or if you treated one person a certain way and somebody else a different way. Start to build yourself up as a reputable business person from the beginning. People will respect you for who you are and how you conduct business.

They will trust you and feel confident in dealing with you. They will also let their acquaintances know about you, and you will pick up even more business. In this day and age, it's hard to find a reputable business, and this can set you apart from the others.

When you go the extra mile to help a person, it doesn't go unnoticed. People enjoy working with others they know are looking out for them. When you have another person's best interest at heart, you'll have a client for life. They will think of you when they need help in the future. They will let others know about you. They will refer you, and that's the best type of advertising a person or business can have.

When you are helping others, you are helping yourself. You not only earn an income from what you like to do, but you can also feel good about doing it. That brings us back to having a sense of purpose in our lives. And fulfilling your sense of purpose creates such a sense of wellbeing that any problems that may crop up in your life will seem to be insignificant.

Information at Your Fingertips

Another good reason for starting a business now is that you can get information at your fingertips, on demand. You can research your subject of interest and see what kind of demand there is for it. You can see what other people do to earn money in your field. You can find holes in that area and fill them. You can fill them with your knowledge or put a little twist into how things are done in that field and become known for that twist.

You will be able to check out your area to see what kind of competition there is for your product or service. You can check to see what other companies charge for the same type of service that you will be providing. It will give you insight as to what you can charge. You may find out there is already a lot of competition, and you may need to change your plans.

You can develop your own niche and become the authority on it. When you develop your own niche, you are the authority. People will come to you for your knowledge and expertise. You can charge whatever you want if there is enough demand and especially if the people that are in demand have money. They will be happy to pay top dollar for your help. You can make it recurring income by offering consultation on a weekly or monthly basis.

If you are going to sell a product, you can shop around for the best prices on the materials that you need. You may need to find a company that can produce your product for you at a better price than what's available now so that you can sell it and make better margins for yourself. That company may help you produce a product that is higher in quality than what's available, and you can take over the competition.

There are many ways that you can get information on the internet that you can use to your advantage. It saves you time, and you can make money.

Let's Talk About Statistics

There's a wide range of statistics about small business. First of all, let's talk about what is considered to be a small business. According to The Small Business Association, a small business makes less than $7,000,000 a year and has fewer than 500 employees. There are a lot of businesses that fit that category. In fact, according to 2007 statistics, there were 27.9 million small businesses in the United States and only 18,500 businesses that had more than 500 employees. I find that amazing.

It seems that we only hear about big business in the news yet it's only a fraction of all the businesses that are out there. There is a total labor force of about 153,000,000 people in the US, and only 13.3 % of the labor force are business owners according to The Bureau of Labor. Still, that equates to over 20,000,000 business owners.

Small business accounts for about 2/3 of new jobs. About half the workforce in the US is employed by small businesses, and small business accounts for close to half of the GDP (Gross Domestic Product.)

There are also some negative statistics about small businesses. About half of the businesses that are started fail in their first year. More fail in their second, third, fourth, and about 95% of those initial businesses are gone by the end of year five. That's not very encouraging, is it? But there are ways to increase your odds of succeeding those five years and surviving beyond year five.

Another interesting fact I want to mention is that about 78.5% of small businesses don't have employees and 52% of small businesses are home-based. 70% of home-based businesses are in construction.

In other words, a lot of people have left the workforce working for other companies and have started a business of their own. And a majority of the people that started their own business are working for themselves and are working out of their own home.

Working out of your own home has many advantages to it. For one, you don't have to lease an office or a building to work from. You don't have to pay rent for your business, and you even get to claim tax write-offs when you work out of your home. If you earn your money working from a computer, you have no commute to work. No commute means that you save a lot of travel time and no wear and tear on your vehicle.

Owning a Home-Based Business

This is the area that I want to focus on. You see, I started my own home-based business in 2004. I started a paint contracting business. When I started, I lived in a 4-plex that I was renting. I had a Datsun pick-up with a canopy that I kept most of my tools in. I built a ladder rack with 2x4's, and there was a basement that I kept some supplies in. In other words, you might say that I started on a shoestring. I had one job lined up when I started, and I didn't even make as much money as I did when I worked for somebody else in my first year.

But I started my own business and had control of my own time. I no longer had to work swing-shifts, graveyard shifts or weekends unless I wanted to. I could pick and choose the jobs I wanted to work on, although I wasn't able to be that choosy when I first started out.

My second year, I made about the same amount of money that I did when I worked for somebody else. I didn't have to work as many hours either. That's because I was able to charge more per hour than what I made as an employee working for somebody else. In fact, I made almost double what I made in the past and sometimes more. I made an average of about $40-$50 per hour.

Working for myself gave me more freedom. It gave me more control over my time. I was able to schedule time off to go on a long deserved vacation. Life was better.

I paid off all my bills and was able to save some money. I got married. My wife encouraged me to start an IRA. We bought a house. I saved some money, and with my wife's encouragement, I bought a rental unit. We were able to go on vacations and go out to restaurants. Life is really good.

You Can Do It!

As I mentioned earlier, you can increase the odds of success when you start your own business. I'm not talking about starting a business with a bunch of employees. I'm talking about starting a business on a shoestring budget so that you can employ yourself. There are millions of people that do this all the time. I want to help you become one of those people.

Just think of it. If you're like me, I dreamed of starting my own business and being my own boss for quite a few years. The dream of owning my own business. The dream of making more money. The dream of more freedom. The dream of more time. The dream of having a life!

The biggest thing that held me up was that I was afraid to start my own business. After all, I had a job with a steady income, and I had no guarantee that I would have success if I started my own business. There is no guarantee of success, but there are ways to reduce the risk of failure.

One way to reduce the risk is to start small. I mean, just start a business so that you can employ yourself. You don't even have to quit your present job when you decide to start your business. You can start by working for yourself on weekends and holidays. You can work after hours from your regular job. You can use any vacation time you might have to work for yourself.

While still working at your present job before you even start on your own, there is a lot of research that should be done. You need to know how much competition there is your area. You should check out the pricing for your area. You should know how much demand there is for your product or service.

If you are going to sell a product, you need to know if supplies are readily available to produce your product. Or, if you are ordering your product pre-assembled, you need to know how long it takes to get your product from the manufacturer. You need to know if you are going to order in a quantity for you to distribute or if you can have your product drop-shipped.

There is a lot of research that can be done before you even move forward with your own business. It's a part of your business planning that should be done so that you know that your proposed business is feasible. The more research that you do before you start, the better your chances are for success. It takes time to conduct all this research and could be done while you are still working for somebody else. If you were just to quit your job and then do the research, you may find yourself without any income for a couple of months while you're checking things out that should have been done before. You could go hungry, or your savings could dwindle down to cover everyday expenses instead of being used as an investment in your new business.

If you are starting a service type of business, you will probably need tools to perform the work required. Using myself as an example, before I started a paint contracting business, I had to have a certain amount of tools before I could get started. I had to have brushes and rollers and roller poles. I had to have ladders and drop cloths. I had to have basic tools like putty knives, screwdrivers, and scrapers. I also had to have basic supplies like tape, plastic, and masking paper. I needed caulk and a caulking gun. It does cost money to have all these tools and supplies, but it really wasn't all that expensive. I already had some of the stuff and to get the rest was only a couple of hundred dollars, a pretty small cost for a start-up.

That was all I needed to get started with interior work. I did interior work for a while, and then I got an exterior job. I had to buy extension ladders, a pressure washer, and a paint sprayer before I could do exterior work. Fortunately, I was able to use a credit card for that which bought me some time, and I was able to pay it off after just a couple of jobs. If I didn't have a credit card, I could've bought these things on Craigslist or rented them from a paint store. There are ways to get started on a shoestring. The total cost of all the equipment I needed for interior and exterior work was less than $2000, and in comparison to how much it might cost to start a bigger business, it's a very small expense. To start a franchise, it could cost you a minimum of $10-20,000, and some franchises could cost hundreds of thousands of dollars, if not millions.

Other businesses need to have an office to accommodate customers. Most city ordinances won't allow you to use your home if you are to have customers walk in through the door. It's disruptive to the neighborhood, and there could be parking issues. So these type of businesses need to lease an office. You would need tables and chairs: a desk and computer and phone services. You need a wide assortment of stationery and office supplies. All these costs add up, and you won't even get an office to begin with unless you have good credit and a fat bank account.

So that's what I'm talking about, starting a small business which can cost thousands of dollars less to start than other businesses out there. You can start with the intention of just employing yourself. After a short amount of time or even after a year or two, you may want to hire somebody to work for you. You go from being self-employed to the employer. More money can be made.

Another advantage of starting a small business is that you will make a profit almost immediately. And by making a profit, I mean that you will be replacing the income that you used to earn working for somebody else in no time at all. You will most likely earn about double the amount per hour than what you used to make. At least that was true in my case.

A larger business may not make a profit for years. A large business may need to get a loan to get an office with all the supplies and be able to make payroll for the employees they would have. And you, as the owner, may not even be able to pay yourself for months. As the owner, you would need to have enough money socked away to survive for months or even longer before your company makes enough money to turn a profit. Then you can get a paycheck yourself. That's the way it is for many larger start-up companies.

Using Your Talent

There are many different types of businesses out there. Most of the owners of a business are expanding their talent to serve the public. They become good at what they do, mostly by working for a company and learning how to perform a certain duty. They become experienced after time. They become skilled and talented.

Once a person becomes talented and experienced in a certain field, they may decide to take that talent and start their own business. Many people are talented in different fields. That's why there are many types of businesses.

You can take your talent and start your own business. You can start your own small business without much worry. Starting a business on a shoestring doesn't put your life in jeopardy. It's worth a try! Even if you lost everything you invested in your start-up company, it's not the end of the world. It's a venture well worth taking. If nothing else you will learn how the business world operates. That's if you fail and a lot of businesses fail before they become successful. They learn how not to do something. That's the worst thing that can happen. You might lose a couple of thousand dollars, but you will have tried. And going through life and not trying something can be worse than not trying at all.

So what if you try and you are successful? It's a great feeling, a sense of accomplishment — a sense of usefulness and purpose by using your talent to help others.

There are so many ways to help others when you start your business. You can use your talent whether you are an artist or weave baskets. Whether you are a cook and sell recipes or you're a gardener and share how you grow delicious vegetables or how to grow flowers. You may be a bookkeeper or a house cleaner. You could be a plumber or a carpenter, a tile setter or a carpet-layer. There are so many fields of work that people are talented in and can use their talents to create their own business.

Some of these businesses can be started with basically no money and can be operated from your home. That's how a vast majority of people earn a living, either owning or working for a small business. Let me tell you, as far as I'm concerned, owning is better than just working for a paycheck. Sure, there might be a bit more responsibility for owning a business, but it can lead to a much more rewarding life. And we haven't even talked about the numerous tax advantages. I'll let you know more about those in an upcoming book.

Sharing your talent and experience and getting paid for it is terrific. When it's also your passion, you may not know whether it's work or play. You have enthusiasm for each day, and it can be quite exciting. You enjoy life.

Let's Review What We've Been Talking About

First, we talked about how working for somebody else or for a company is not as secure as it once had been. You could lose your job at any time for a number of different reasons. We also discussed how you can also learn from the business you are in and how you can stay alert and keep your eyes open for an opportunity that can be created. We talked about how you might be able to improve a product in demand or perform a better service than the company you work for now.

We also talked about how you can help other people accomplish their dreams and desires. And how you can teach them how to fulfill those dreams by teaching them with the skills and knowledge that you have. By teaching them, you have a more meaningful life. You give of yourself to them, and you earn money while doing it. That can lead to more financial security for yourself and adds to your own sense of purpose in life.

We also discussed some of the statistics of small business and how you can reduce the odds of failure. The first way to increase your chances of success is to conduct research. You can research the ins and outs of other businesses in your area of expertise. You can learn about the supply and demand and the amounts charged for the service or product that you will be providing.

We mentioned the reasons why a small home-based business is practical; it's much less expensive to operate, and you can even get tax breaks from the IRS. It's relatively inexpensive to start your own business home-based especially compared to starting other small businesses or franchises. We talked about how you can start a business and just keep yourself employed, and how you can expand in the future if that is what you desire.

We talked about some of the benefits of running your own business. You can earn a higher hourly rate than what you used to make. You are allowed to set your own schedule. You have more freedom.

But most importantly, you are helping other people to become successful. You are sharing your talents and skills. You have a higher sense of purpose and live a more meaningful life. Your life is more satisfying when you share your knowledge to help other people fulfill their dreams.

What's next?

So you learned how to start a successful small home-based business and actually moved ahead and did it. You started to earn more money and started to invest it. You bought yourself a house and started a Roth IRA. You have accumulated some money and a few assets.

Now you need to know how to keep it!

You need to know how to **"Cover Your A$$ - How to Protect Yourself from the Low-Life Blood-Sucking Parasites That Want to Sue You" (It's Their Way to Acquire Wealth at Your Expense!),** the title to my next book.

It's about what you can do to protect yourself, your family, and your business from being sued. In this day and age where people are out there looking for a reason to sue somebody as a means to get money, you need to protect yourself. There are some things that you can do to protect yourself from being sued and minimize the risk of losing what you have worked a lifetime to earn.

To get a copy when it becomes available, go to my website   www.yourhigherdesire.com

About the Author

I'm Russell DeBord, The creator of "Your Higher Desire, LLC." My purpose is to share my experience in life with you so that you can improve your life. I want to help you achieve "Your Higher Desire" in your life.

My hope is to help you succeed with your wants and desires. You can learn from my mistakes and not repeat them. I hope to share what I have learned so that you can save time. You can get off to a quicker start with your endeavors.

I grew up in the State of Washington. I'm a third-generation painter and worked as an industrial painter for about ten years. I did commercial painting for another ten years and then got into residential painting. I started my own paint contracting business in 2004 and am still contracting to this date.

I'm getting a bit older now and am shifting my talent to writing, getting away from physical labor. My goal is to share my experience with you so that you may succeed in your life as I have in mine.

My wife, Virginia, and I moved to and have been residing in Mesa, Arizona since 2016.

Thank You!

I want to personally thank you for reading my book. I invite you to express your views and thoughts about the book. You can help influence and improve the next book that I write by sharing what you think was positive about the book and also how it may have been better.

You can help influence me, or any other author of their book, by letting us know your feelings about what you read by writing a review. With your feedback, you let us know what we did right and where we might need to make adjustments.

Reviews are the heartbeat of journalism and even products that are produced. Many people don't make a decision to purchase a thing without first reading the reviews. So, you can help influence the way this whole economy works by giving your opinion about a book or product.

Didn't know you had so much power, did you?

So, go ahead and leave a review and make a difference in this world!

Thank You, Russell

Click here to leave a review. https://www.amazon.com/dp/B07RHVVLCX

www.ingramcontent.com/pod-product-compliance
Lightning Source LLC
Chambersburg PA
CBHW031941170526
45157CB00008B/3263